MIGHTY ANIMAL MIGRATIONS

A WILDEBEEST'S JOURNEY

David and Julie Lavender

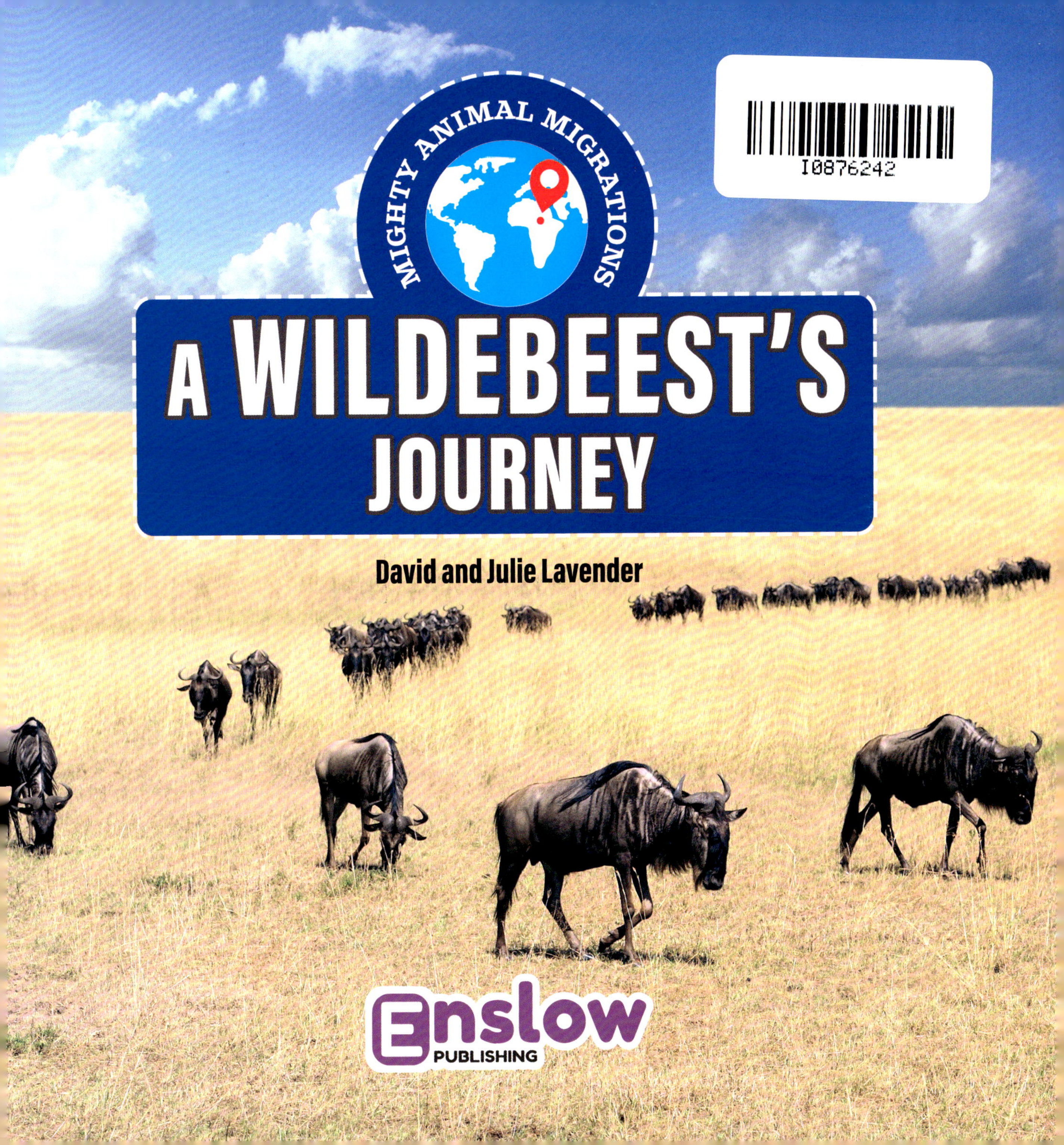

Enslow PUBLISHING

Please visit our website, www.enslow.com. For a free color catalog of all our high-quality books, call toll free 1-800-398-2504 or fax 1-877-980-4454

Published in 2027 by
Enslow Publishing
2544 Clinton Street
Buffalo, NY 14224

Cataloging-in-Publication Data
Names: Lavender, David R., 1961-, author. | Lavender, Julie, author.
Title: A wildebeest's journey / by David and Julie Lavender.
Description: Buffalo, NY : Enslow Publishing, 2027. | Series: Mighty animal migrations | Includes glossary.
Identifiers: ISBN 9781978549661 (pbk.) | ISBN 9781978549678 (library bound) | ISBN 9781978549685 (ebook)
Subjects: LCSH: Gnus--Migration--Juvenile literature.
Classification: LCC QL737.U53 L384 2027 | DDC 599.64591568--dc23

Photo credits: Cover, p 1, Volodymyr Burdiak/Shutterstock.com; Calendars used throught interior, Evolvect/AdobeStock.com; background used throughout interior, lovelyday12/AdobeStock.com; p 4, Jane Rix/Shutterstock.com; p 5, Arab/Shutterstock.com, Robert Harding Video/Shutterstock.com; p 6, costas anton dumitrescu/Shutterstock.com; p 7, KensCanning/Shutterstock.com; p 8, JulianBuijzen/Shutterstock.com; p 9, RujStudio/Shutterstock.com; p 10, Sergey Uryadnikov/Shutterstock.com; p 11, Todd Grimsely/Shutterstock.com; p 12, Martin Mecnarowski/Shutterstock.com; p 13, Martens Coyotes/Shutterstock.com; p 14, Maurizio Bersanelli/Shutterstock.com; p 15, Budimir Jevtic/Shutterstock.com; p 16, Hawatrending/Shutterstock.com; p 17, godongphoto/Shutterstock.com; p 18, pornpoj/Shutterstock.com; p 19, Pavel Chepelev/Shutterstock.com, GUIDO BISSATTINI/Shutterstock.com; p 21, punitbhatia/Shutterstock.com; p 22, EcoPrint/Shutterstock.com; p 23, Nick Dale Photo/Shutterstock.com, Marie-Anne AbersonM/Shutterstock.com; P 24, AndreAnita/Shutterstock.com; p 25, Joe McDonald/Shutterstock.com, Maurizio Bersanelli/Shutterstock.com; p 26, Beate Wolter/Shutterstock.com; p 27, Tyrone Winfield/Shutterstock.com; p 28, 29, Luka Veselinovic/Shutterstock.com

Printed in China

CPSIA compliance information: Batch #CSENS27: For further information, contact Enslow Publishing, New York, New York, at 1-800-398-2504.

Table of Contents

Moving Onward

Millions of animals migrate every year over land, sea, or air.

They set out on long, dangerous journeys. Sometimes animals migrate to find a mate or a place to birth their young. Sometimes they search for food or better weather conditions. For wildebeests, hunger and thirst push them to keep going.

More than one million blue wildebeests travel 500 miles (800 km) or more each year. Many won't survive. They face lions, cheetahs, and leopards on land. They encounter hippos and crocodiles in rivers. They face many dangers. But they press onward!

blue wildebeest

black wildebeest

Have You Herd?

The two types of wildebeest are the blue (or common) wildebeest and the black (or white-tailed) wildebeest. Adults can weigh up to 600 pounds (272 kg).

A Wildebeest Is Born

One February morning, a wildebeest calf is born in the short grass of the southern Serengeti Plain in Tanzania. Its long, rectangular head nuzzles close to its mother to nurse. She licks him clean. A strong bond forms between them. This will be important in the difficult days ahead.

The new calf must stand quickly. Hyenas and cheetahs lurk nearby. In just minutes, the wildebeest pushes up on thin, wobbly legs. He stands close to his mother for protection.

Ten days later, the calf nibbles on grass for the first time. He will continue to drink his mother's milk for up to nine months.

Have You Herd?

Pregnant wildebeests give birth between January and March. Most wildebeests have their calves within the same two to three weeks in February. A newborn calf weighs 40 pounds (18 kg).

Migration Begins

The rainy season ends in the southern Serengeti. Grass shrivels and dries up. The wildebeests' main food source is gone. It's time for the herd to migrate in search of fresh grass to eat.

Millions of hooves make their way west. The two-month-old wildebeest calf sticks close to his mother.

Zebras and gazelles join the wildebeest in the great migration. There is safety in numbers. **Predators** are never far away.

Have You Herd?

Migrating wildebeests move across the Serengeti National Park in Tanzania and the Masai Mara National Reserve in Kenya.

The River of Terror

Coarse grass grows on rolling hills in the **savanna**. Acacia trees dot the landscape. Lions prowl atop huge boulders. They hope to snatch a lone calf. Leopards watch from tree branches for their next meal.

The herd **grazes** as it moves north. The wildebeests get ready to cross the Grumeti River. At just the right moment, the young wildebeest leaps into the river next to his mother.

He kicks and pushes forward. The current moves fast. It's hard to fight against the swift water. A crocodile grabs a wildebeest nearby and pulls it under. The wildebeest calf swims faster.

Mating Season

Tired. Weak. Weary. Scared. But finally, the young wildebeest is on the other side. His mother pushes him up the riverbank of the Grumeti River. She knows cheetahs may hide in the tall grass. The predators wait for exhausted wildebeests in hopes of a hearty dinner for their own survival.

Rain on the other side of the river allows **nutrient**-rich grass to carpet the Grumeti Reserve. The young wildebeest grazes hungrily. He quickly regains strength and energy.

The young wildebeest watches males bash heads and horns together. Mating season has arrived. New wildebeests will be born eight months later.

River Dangers

More than one million hungry wildebeests graze on every blade of green grass. They continue to move north toward greener grass and new rain. The Mara River offers fresh water for thirsty wildebeests. But it brings danger too.

Thundering hooves rush into the muddy water. The young wildebeest leaps and scrambles. He doesn't want to get squashed by the herd.

Hippopotamuses grunt and charge. The huge animals force the wildebeests away. Crocodiles snap and grab with razor-sharp teeth. The young wildebeest fights his way to the other side.

Have You Herd?

Hippopotamuses like to claim their living area. They are territorial. This means they protect their space fiercely and won't share it.

Another Country

Wildebeests that survive the river step into a new country. Lush, green grass blankets the Masai Mara National Reserve in Kenya. Tall trees offer shade.

A loud roar alarms the wildebeests. Suddenly, a lion dashes into the herd. The wildebeests scatter. This time, the lion loses. The young wildebeest is safe.

Wildlife Abounds

The Masai Mara is home to many animals. Some are threats to the wildebeests, but not all. African bush elephants roam the Masai Mara. Buffalo and giraffes graze here too. Black rhinoceroses struggle to survive.

Birds like storks and hornbills search for food. Eagles and hawks soar high and nest in tall trees.

The young wildebeest is uneasy with the strange new creatures. Aardvarks, hares, mongooses, monkeys, porcupines, and others mingle with the wildebeest herd.

Have You Herd?

Poachers have killed so many black rhinoceroses for their horns that this large mammal is **endangered.**

The Rains Return

Instinct tells the wildebeests that rains have returned in the south. The massive herd starts its march back to the plains of the Serengeti. The wildebeests separate into family groups and graze on the way south.

The young wildebeest doesn't need the protection of his mother now. He travels alongside other young male wildebeests. But he remains **vigilant**. One wrong move and he could be a leopard's lunch.

Back Where He Started

Gentle drops of rain soak the dry ground. New shoots appear. Green grasses cover the plains once again.

The wildebeest practices fighting with other young males. He pushes up on his back legs. He rams his head against another wildebeest. Their horns are still too small to be dangerous.

Have You Herd?

Male and female wildebeests have thick, curved horns with sharp points. They can grow to be more than two feet (61 cm) long. Calves are born without horns. Their horns won't be fully grown for three years.

The Cycle Begins Anew

Green grass grows as far as the eye can see. Wildebeests spread out to graze across the open plains. Puddles form from the fresh rain. Drinking water is plentiful.

Without the safety of the herd, wildebeests risk an **ambush** from hyenas or cheetahs. The year-old wildebeest scans the **horizon** for threats.

The wildebeest notices pregnant females gathered close together. Other wildebeests form a wall around them as protection. Soon, new wildebeest calves will be born. Life will begin again.

The Wildebeest Migration

The wildebeest has survived his first migration. The Great Wildebeest Migration cycle will continue every year. The mighty mammals must migrate or starve to death. Rains that bring fresh water and lush grass urge them along the journey.

Yet many will die during the migration from predators, illness, or sheer exhaustion.

Those that complete the harsh journey maintain the wildebeest population. They'll help support a healthy **ecosystem**. And they'll be part of one of the largest animal migrations on Earth.

Have You Herd?

One million pooping wildebeests have a huge impact on the ecosystem. Wildebeests' poop fertilizes the soil and provides important nutrients for new grass.

The Great Wildebeest Migration Map

1. Life begins in the short grass plains in the southern tip of Serengeti National Park. The Great Wildebeest Migration begins when calves are just a few months old.

2. Moving clockwise, the herd of more than one million wildebeests marches west to the long grass plains. Often, the line of wildebeests stretches for miles and miles.

3. After crossing the Grumeti River in the western edge of the Serengeti, the wildebeests travel north. They'll cross another river, the Mara River, to graze in the Masai Mara National Reserve.

4. Rain returns to the Serengeti, and the herd travels south. Another migration cycle ends. Yet the search for fresh grass and water is never-ending. Millions of stomping hooves signal the next migration ...

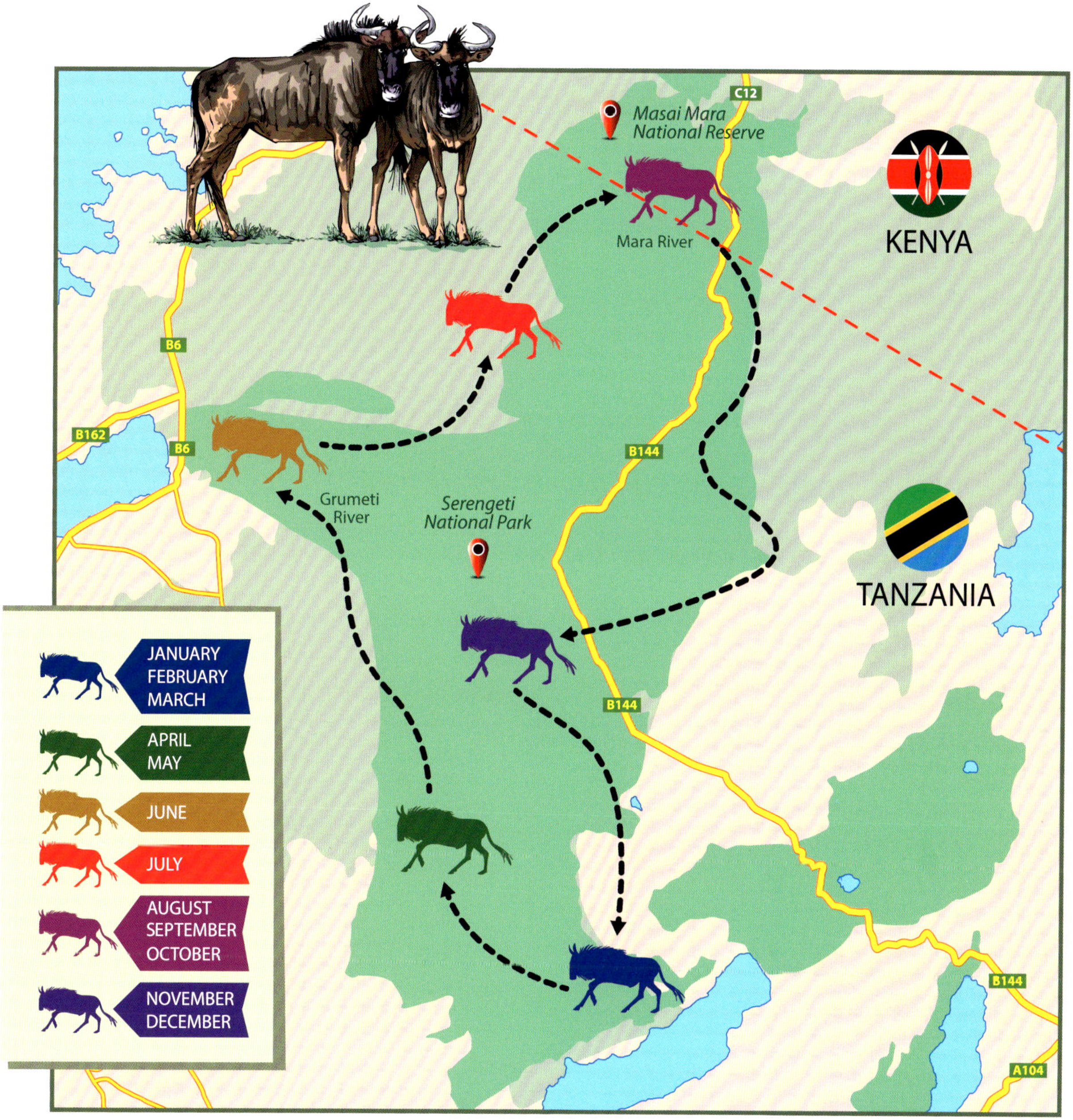
C12
Masai Mara
National Reserve
KENYA
Mara River
B6
B162
B6
B144
Grumeti
River
Serengeti
National Park
TANZANIA
B144
B144
A104
JANUARY
FEBRUARY
MARCH
APRIL
MAY
JUNE
JULY
AUGUST
SEPTEMBER
OCTOBER
NOVEMBER
DECEMBER

Glossary

ambush (AM-bush): to attack an animal from a hiding place

ecosystem (EE-koh-sis-tuhm): all the living things in a place and their relation to their environment

endangered (en-DAYN-jurd): a species that is in danger of becoming extinct

grazes (GRAYZ-iz): eats grass that is growing in a field or on a plain

horizon (huh-RYE-zuhn): the line where the earth seems to meet the sky

instinct (IN-stingkt): behavior that is natural and not learned

nutrient (NOO-tree-uhnt): something that is needed by animals and plants to stay strong and healthy, like proteins, minerals, and vitamins

poachers (POH-churz): people who hunt illegally on someone else's land

predators (PRED-uh-turz): animals that live by hunting other animals for food

savanna (suh-VAN-uh): a flat, grassy plain with few or no trees

vigilant (VIJ-uh-luhnt): watchful and alert

Fact Check

1. Wildebeests must cross rivers quickly to avoid being eaten by ________.

   a. lions b. snakes c. crocodiles

2. Wildebeests migrate in search of fresh water and _____.

   a. grass b. oats c. corn

3. Some wildebeests do not survive the migration because of ______, illness, or exhaustion.

   a. heat b. predators c. getting lost

Answers: 1. c, 2. a, 3. b

Further Reading

Bradley, Doug. *Animal Migration*. Britannica Educational Publishing, 2023.

Gieseke, Tyler. *Migration Cycles*. ABDO Publishing Company, 2022.

MacCarald, Clara. *Migrating to Survive*. ABDO Publishing Company, 2022.

On the Internet

Wildebeests

www.ifaw.org/animals/wildebeests

Read more about wildebeests' eating habits, migration patterns, and benefits to the ecosystem.

Wildebeest

www.awf.org/wildlife-conservation/wildebeest

Explore this site to learn more about wildebeests' behaviors, diet, and habitat.

Publisher's note to educators and parents: Our editors have carefully reviewed these websites to ensure that they are suitable for students. Many websites change frequently, however, and we cannot guarantee that a site's future contents will continue to meet our high standards of quality and educational value. Be advised that students should be closely supervised whenever they access the internet.

Index

About the Authors

While working as an entomologist for the United States Navy, David witnessed the Great Wildebeest Migration at Masai Mara in Kenya. He's been fascinated with animal migrations ever since then! David worked as a wildlife biologist for the Army too. Julie is a former public school teacher and homeschooling mom. They are the parents of four and grandparents of three. They love getting outside and admiring the wonders of animals and nature, and then writing about them. Julie and David have written books about sharks, leopards, lemurs and other animals, hidden treasure, and a picture book called *A Gingerbread House*.